The Orchard Book of
GREEK MYTHS

The Orchard Book of
GREEK MYTHS

Geraldine McCaughrean

Illustrated by Emma Chichester Clark

ORCHARD BOOKS

First published in Great Britain in 1992 by
ORCHARD BOOKS
96 Leonard Street, London EC2A 4RH
Orchard Books Australia
14 Mars Road, Lane Cove, NSW 2066
Text © Geraldine McCaughrean 1992
Illustrations © Emma Chichester Clark 1992
The right of Geraldine McCaughrean to be identified as author of this work and of Emma Chichester Clark
as illustrator has been asserted by them in accordance with the Copyright, Designs and Patents Act, 1988.
A CIP catalogue record for this book is available from the British Library.
1 85213 373 2
Printed in Malaysia

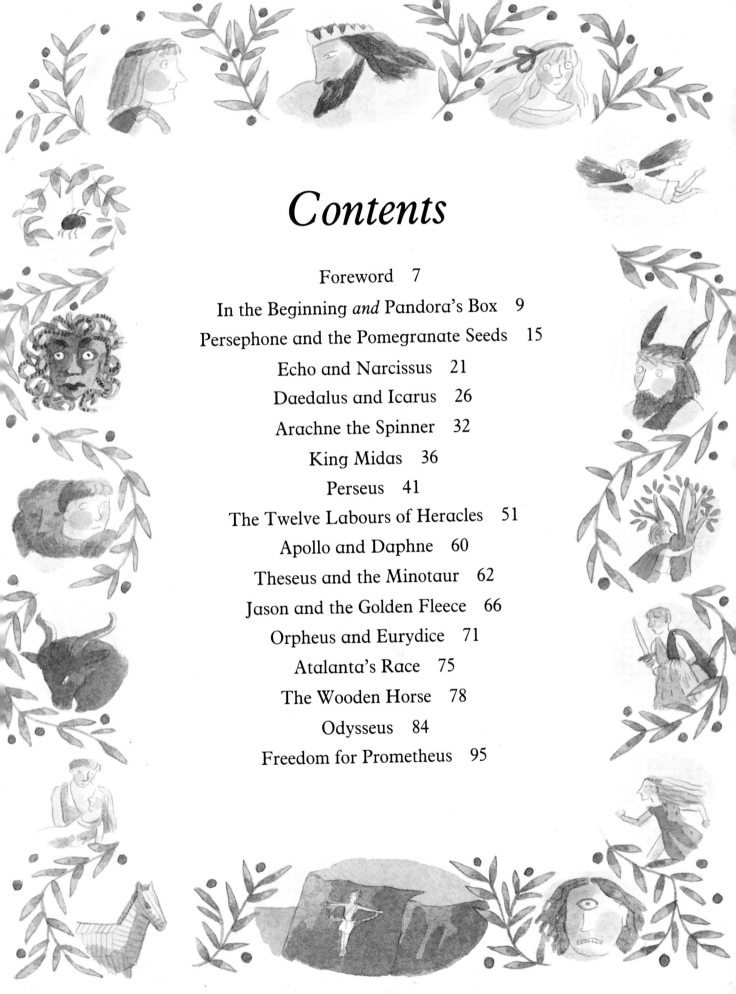

Contents

For Sophie Victoria Drasodomska Jones
G.M.

For Mark and Sophia
E.C.C.

Foreword

When these stories were first told, three thousand years ago, they were much, much more than stories. They were, for the Ancient Greeks, a way of making sense of the world – how it began, why summer gives way to autumn and the leaves fall, why some people are lucky and some are not, what becomes of man after he dies . . .

The Ancient Greeks believed that high up, on the top of the highest mountain in the country, sat a family of gods. One was in charge of the sea, whipping up storms and frightening sailors. Another ripened the harvest in the fields. One could shoot arrows of love into the stoniest heart. Another decided the winning side in a war. In fact, every aspect of life was looked after by one of those immortal gods living on Mount Olympus.

But far from being perfect and full of wisdom, the gods in the Greek heaven were just as silly as us. They squabbled, they fell in love, they played tricks on each other and on the people in their care. They chased pretty women, helped handsome heroes, and dressed up in all kinds of disguises. They were vain, jealous, spiteful, bad-tempered – even lonely. And mixed in with stories of these gods were others – half-remembered adventures of legendary Greeks whose deeds grew in the telling into adventures worthy of any immortal god.

So why, when we no longer believe there are gods living at the top of Mount Olympus, are we still telling their stories? Because they are full of the things that fascinate anyone, in any country, at any time. There are adventures and jokes, fables and fairy stories, thrills and happy endings. In short, the Greek myths are just too good to forget.

Geraldine McCaughrean

In the Beginning and Pandora's Box

At the very beginning, the gods ruled over an empty world. From their home on Mount Olympus, where they lived in halls of sunlight and cloud, they looked out over oceans and islands, woodland and hill. But nothing moved in the landscape because there were no animals or birds or people.

Zeus, king of the gods, gave Prometheus and his brother Epimetheus the task of making living creatures, and he sent them down to live on earth. Epimetheus made turtles and gave them shells; he made horses and gave them tails and manes. He made anteaters and gave them long noses and longer tongues; he made birds and gave them the gift of flight. But although Epimetheus was a wonderful craftsman, he was not nearly as clever as his brother. So Prometheus watched over his brother's work and, when all the animals and birds, insects and fishes were made, it was Prometheus who made the very last creature of all. He took soil and mixed it into mud, and out of that he moulded First Man.

"I'll make him just like us gods—two legs, two arms and upright—not crawling on all fours. All the other beasts spend their days looking at the ground, but Man will look at the stars!"

When he had finished, Prometheus was very proud of what he had made. But when it came to giving Man a gift, there was nothing left to give!

"Give him a tail," said Epimetheus. But all the tails had gone. "Give him a trunk," Epimetheus suggested. But the elephant already had that. "Give him fur," said Epimetheus, but all the fur had been used up.

Suddenly Prometheus exclaimed, "I know what to give him!" He climbed up to heaven—up as high as the fiery chariot of the sun. And from the rim of its bright wheel he stole one tiny sliver of fire. It was such a very small flame that he was able to hide it inside a stalk of grass and hurry back to the earth without any of the gods seeing what he was up to.

But the secret could not be kept for long. Next time Zeus looked down from Mount Olympus, he saw something glimmering red and yellow under a column of grey smoke.

"Prometheus, what have you done? You've given the secret of fire to those . . . those . . . mud-men! Bad enough that you make them look like gods, now you go sharing our belongings with them! So! You put your little mud-people before us, do you? I'll make you sorry you ever made them! I'll make you sorry you were ever made yourself!"

And he tied Prometheus to a cliff and sent eagles to peck at him all day long. You or I would have died. But the gods can never die. Prometheus knew that the pain would never end, that the eagles would never stop and that his chains would never break. A terrible hopelessness tore at his heart and hurt him more than the eagles could ever do.

Zeus was just as angry with Man for *accepting* the gift of fire, but you would never have thought so. He was busy making him another wonderful present.

With the help of the other gods, he shaped First Woman. Venus gave her beauty, Mercury gave her a clever tongue, Apollo taught her how to play sweet music. Finally Zeus draped a veil over her lovely head and named her Pandora.

Then, with a grin on his face, he sent for Epimetheus (who was not quite clever enough to suspect a trick).

"Here's a bride for you, Epimetheus—a reward for all your hard work making the animals. And here's a wedding present for you both. But whatever you do, don't open it."

The wedding present was a wooden chest, bolted and padlocked and

bound with bands of iron. When he reached his home at the foot of Mount Olympus, Epimetheus set the chest down in a dark corner, covered it with a blanket, and put it out of his mind. After all, with Pandora for a bride, what more could a man possibly want?

In those days the world was a wonderful place to live. No one was sad. Nobody ever grew old or ill. And Epimetheus married Pandora; she came to live in his house, and everything she wanted he gave her.

But sometimes, when she caught sight of the chest, Pandora would say, "What a strange wedding present. Why can't we open it?"

"Never mind why. Remember, you must never touch it," Epimetheus would reply sharply. "Not touch at all. Do you hear?"

"Of course I won't touch it. It's only an old chest. What do I want with an old chest? . . . What do you think is inside?"

"Never mind what's inside. Put it out of your mind."

And Pandora did try. She really did. But one day, when Epimetheus was out, she just could not forget about the chest and somehow she found herself standing right beside it.

"No!" she told herself. "I expect it's full of cloth—or dishes—or papers.

11

Something dull." She bustled about the house. She tried to read. Then . . .

"*Let us out!*"

"Who said that?"

"Do let us out, Pandora!"

Pandora looked out of the window. But in her heart of hearts she knew that the voice was coming from the chest. She pulled back the blanket with finger and thumb. The voice was louder now: "Please, please *do* let us out, Pandora!"

"I can't. I mustn't." She crouched down beside the chest.

"Oh, but you *have* to. We *want* you to. We *need* you to, Pandora!"

"But I promised!" Her fingers stroked the latch.

"It's easy. The key's in the lock," said the little voice—a purring little voice.

It was. A big golden key.

"No. No, I mustn't," she told herself.

"But you do *want* to, Pandora. And why shouldn't you? It was your wedding present too, wasn't it? . . . Oh, all right, don't let us out. Just peep inside. What harm can that do?"

Pandora's heart beat faster.

Click. The key turned.

Clack. Clack. The latches were unlatched.

BANG!

The lid flew back and Pandora was knocked over by an icy wind full of grit. It filled the room with howling. It tore the curtains and stained them brown. And after the wind came slimy things, growling snarling things, claws and snouts, revolting things too nasty to look at, all slithering out of the chest.

"I'm Disease," said one.

"I'm Cruelty," said another.

"I'm Pain, and she's Old Age."

"I'm Disappointment and he's Hate."

"I'm Jealousy and that one there is War."

"AND I AM DEATH!" said the smallest purring voice.

The creatures leapt and scuttled and oozed out through the windows, and at once all the flowers shrivelled, and the fruit on the trees grew mouldy. The sky itself turned a filthy yellow, and the sound of crying filled the town.

Mustering all her strength, Pandora slammed down the lid of the chest. But there was one creature left inside.

"No, no, Pandora! If you shut me inside, that will be your worst mistake of all! Let me go!"

"Oh no! You don't fool me twice," sobbed Pandora.

"But I am Hope!" whispered the little voice faintly. "Without me the world won't be able to bear all the unhappiness you have turned loose!"

So Pandora lifted the lid, and a white flicker, small as a butterfly, flitted out and was blown this way and that by the howling winds. And as it fluttered through the open window, a watery sun came out and shone on the wilted garden.

Chained to his cliff, Prometheus could do nothing to help the little mud-people he had made. Though he writhed and strained, there was no breaking free. All around him he could hear the sound of crying. Now that the snarling creatures had been let loose, there would be no more easy days or peaceful nights for men and women! They would be unkind, afraid, greedy, unhappy. And one day they must all die and go to live as ghosts in the cold dark Underworld. The thought of it almost broke Prometheus' heart.

Then, out of the corner of his eye, he glimpsed a little white flicker of light and felt something, small as a butterfly, touch his bare breast. Hope came to rest over his heart.

He felt a sudden strength, a sort of courage. He was sure that his life was not over. "No matter how bad things are today, tomorrow may be better," he thought. "One day someone may come this way—take pity on me— break these chains and set me free. One day!"

The eagles pecked at the fluttering shred of light but were too slow to catch it in their beaks. Hope fluttered on its way, blowing round the world like a single tiny tongue of flame.

Persephone and the Pomegranate Seeds

In those early days the weather was always warm and sunny. The flowers were always in bloom, the crops were always ready for harvest. The goddess Demeter tended the countryside like a garden, planting seeds, watering the green grass, encouraging the trees to put on first blossom, then leaves, then fruit.

And while Demeter worked, her little daughter Persephone used to play in the green woods of Sicily, picking violets until her apron was full. When mother and child walked home hand in hand at the end of another sunny day, talking and singing and laughing together, the evening primroses opened just to watch them pass by.

Pluto was not so lucky. Although he was a god, he did not live on the top of Mount Olympus in halls of cloud and sunlight, or on the earth among trees and fields. Pluto ruled over the Kingdom of the Dead, and lived under the earth in darkness and bitter cold. Not one ray of sunshine ever found its way down into those echoing caverns and tunnels.

But worse than either cold or dark was the loneliness. Pluto tried to find a wife, but nobody wanted to give up the sunshine, the flowers, or the glittering sea to live in Pluto's dismal kingdom beneath the ground. Sometimes Pluto would climb to the brim of the Underworld and peep out at the girls and women playing in the sun. The bright light hurt his eyes, but the sight of all those pretty women hurt even more.

One day he saw Persephone picking violets in her Sicilian wood.

"That's the one," murmured Pluto. "How beautiful she is! Oh yes, she's the wife for me."

But Pluto did not go to Demeter and ask to marry her daughter: he knew she would say no. Instead, he harnessed his black chariot and thundered out into the sunlight. Lashing his whip, he drove his horses on at full tilt. All Sicily shook at his coming, and his wheels felled trees to right and left as he raced through the woods. Holding the reins in his teeth, Pluto leaned out and snatched Persephone by her long hair. Her apron spilled all its violets.

"Who are you? What do you want with me? Oh let me go! Help me, somebody! Mother, help me!" she cried.

The trees bawled after Pluto, "Come back! Leave her alone!" Their green leaves flushed red with shouting, but Pluto took no notice as he raced back to his Underworld. He struck out with his whip. The earth split open. A bottomless ravine gaped, and his chariot sped downwards. Down into the dark, down into the cold, he carried Persephone.

"Don't cry," he told her. "I shall make you my queen. Be happy! I'll give you all the riches of the earth—gold and silver and gems! You have the love of a king! What more do you want?"

"I want to go home! I want my mother!" sobbed Persephone.

16

PERSEPHONE AND THE POMEGRANATE SEEDS

When they reached the River Styx, which divides the earth from the Kingdom of the Dead, she cried out, "River, help me! I am Persephone! Save me, please!"

The river heard her and knotted itself around the god's legs, almost tripping him. But Pluto kicked it aside like a dog. In despair, Persephone slipped off her belt of flowers and threw it into the tumbling water. "Take that to my mother and tell her!" she pleaded. The river took her belt and hurried away. Then darkness closed in on all sides: Pluto had reached home with his captive wife.

Meanwhile, up on the earth, Demeter came looking for her daughter at the end of the day.

"Persephone darling! Time to go home!"

But there was no answer. Demeter called out and asked everyone she met, but it was hopeless. Persephone had simply disappeared.

All Demeter's work was forgotten as she searched high and low for the child. Nothing mattered but to find Persephone. So the flowers wilted. The crops stopped growing. And as Demeter wept, the trees wept with her, shedding their leaves in brown and yellow tears.

After searching the world over, Demeter returned to Sicily and sat down in despair beside a river. As she gazed at the water, what should come spinning by on the current but a little cord of flowers.

"Persephone is in the Underworld," whispered the water. "I saw her! Pluto has stolen her away to be his queen."

Then Demeter ran all the way to Mount Olympus and rattled at the gates of heaven. "Zeus! Lord Zeus! Help me! Pluto has stolen away my daughter! Make him give her back!"

Zeus listened to poor Demeter. "You say your daughter was taken by force? Pluto shouldn't have done that. But there again—"

"Oh, Zeus!" she interrupted him. "If I don't get my daughter back, how shall I go on decking the earth with flowers and fruit? I only do it out of joy, and without Persephone there is no joy for me! Let the earth wither and die for all I care!"

Zeus shivered at the thought. The little people on the earth would quickly stop paying tribute to the gods if their crops stopped growing and their trees died.

"It's not up to me," he said gruffly. "There are rules. If Persephone eats anything while she is in the Underworld, she cannot come back up to the earth. That's the rule."

"Then what are you waiting for?" said Demeter. "Send your messenger this instant!"

And though Zeus sent Hermes, fastest flying of all the gods, Demeter sped ahead of him that day, pulling on his sleeve, begging him to hurry.

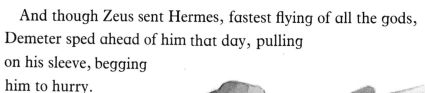

Meanwhile, below the earth, Pluto laid in front of Persephone a delicious feast. He knew (what she did not) that if she ate one mouthful she must stay with him for ever.

"I'm too miserable to eat," sobbed Persephone. "Let me go. Why don't you let me go? It's so dark and gloomy here!"

Pluto no longer thought his kingdom was dark or gloomy. Now that Persephone sat on a throne beside his, it seemed bright and cheerful. Hosts of ghosts came streaming through the darkness to gaze at his new bride. Pluto was very happy indeed.

"But you must eat, my dear. Just try a little something." He held up a dish of limes, an almond cake, a cup of broth, tempting her to eat.

"I'd rather die than eat your food," said Persephone, even though she was very, very hungry.

"Just a little taste." Pluto held up a half pomegranate—all red and juicy, smiling with seeds. He forced open her fingers and sprinkled twelve seeds into her palm.

Oh and she was so very hungry! For days she had sat and pined, hoping her mother might find her. But her mother did not come and did not come. Persephone was too hungry to think. She lifted the seeds to her lips . . .

"Stop!"

Hermes, messenger of the gods, came skimming through the air in his winged sandals. "Noble Pluto! Zeus the Almighty commands you to let Persephone go . . . Or am I too late?" He looked at the feast laid out in front of the two thrones.

"Yes, yes! You're too late!" crowed Pluto.

"No, no! What do you mean?" cried Persephone. Six little pomegranate seeds fell from the palm of her hand.

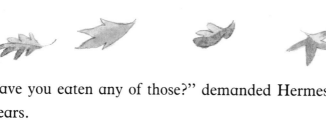

"Have you eaten any of those?" demanded Hermes. Persephone burst into tears.

"She has! She has!" cried Pluto triumphantly. "She's mine for ever!"

"Only a few!" pleaded Persephone. "What difference does it make?"

"Pluto, you're a rascal," said Hermes. "You should have told her. I'm sorry, Persephone. There's a rule, you see. You have accepted Pluto's hospitality—eaten his food. So now you must stay here for ever."

"*And hate you for ever, Pluto!*" cried Persephone, "*because you tricked me!*"

When she said this, even Pluto turned a little pale. He loved Persephone and wanted her to love him in return. "I only stole you away because I was so lonely," he said, hanging his head.

Hermes felt sorry for them both. "Let Zeus decide!" he declared.

When Zeus heard what had happened, he thought long and hard before making his judgement. Finally, he declared, "Because Persephone ate six of the twelve pomegranate seeds, let her live for six months of every year in the Kingdom of the Dead. For the other six months let her live with her mother, on the earth . . . And let no one argue with the judgement of Zeus!"

And that is why, in the summertime, the flowers bloom, the grass is green and the trees wear blossom, then leaves, then fruit. Demeter, you see, is rushing happily here and there, tending the earth like a garden. When she and her daughter walk hand in hand, talking and singing and laughing, the evening primroses open just to see them pass by.

But in the autumn, Persephone travels down to the Underworld, to keep her bargain with Pluto. First she learned to pity him. Then she learned to love him. And now the Underworld is much brighter and warmer during the six winter months. But up on the earth Demeter is missing her daughter. The trees flush red with calling Persephone's name, then drop their leaves. The flowers wither. The crops stop growing and the earth and the people of the earth wait for Persephone to return with the spring.

Echo and Narcissus

All the goddesses liked to run through the silent woods on Mount Olympus, playing and chasing the deer. There was Queen Hera, soundless as the sun's rays; there was Diana, quiet as moonlight; there were the wood nymphs flitting like thistledown . . . and then there was Echo.

Echo was always chattering, arguing or shrieking with laughter. The deer scattered as soon as Echo opened her mouth.

"Echo!" said Hera sternly to her one day. "You've done it again!"

"What? Didn't do anything," said Echo pertly.

"Yes you did. You talked. You're always talking."

"I'm not!"

"You are. Don't tell me you're not."

"Not," said Echo, who always had to have the last word. "Not, not, not."

Hera was so angry that she pointed a magic finger at Echo. "Once and for all, be silent!"

The nymph was struck dumb. She put her hands to her throat, her fingers to her lips, and looked around in horror.

"Let this be a lesson to you. You always wanted the last word. Now you shall have nothing else!"

" . . . nothing else," said Echo. She found the words in her mouth, and they were the only ones she could speak.

"You may go now," said the queen of the gods.

21

" . . . go now," said Echo, without meaning to.

Echo ran sobbing off the mountain and wandered about miserably in the foothills. There, amid his flock of sheep, she saw a shepherd boy. He was combing his curly hair into ringlets and brushing the grass off his tunic. This was Narcissus, and Narcissus was as beautiful as any god. The shepherdesses could not lay eyes on him without falling in love.

Echo was no different from the shepherdesses. She fell in love with Narcissus at first sight, and what she would have given to be able to tell him so! But her lips were sealed like a locked door. All she could do was follow him about, her hands full of flowers and her eyes full of love.

"What can I do for you?" he asked, when he saw her gazing at him.

" . . . for you . . . for you," said Echo, and laid the flowers at his feet.

Unfortunately, Narcissus was quite used to women falling in love with him. It happened all the time. He knew how handsome he was and that made him very, very vain. Worse still, he did not much like women, did not want their sickly, syrupy love. Echo only annoyed him, trailing along behind him, saying nothing, staring with her mouth open.

"Everywhere I go, you follow," he complained.

" . . . follow . . . follow," said Echo.

"Stupid girl. I suppose you think you love me."

" . . . love me . . . love me," pleaded Echo.

"You bore me. Leave me alone!"

" . . . alone! alone!" wailed Echo. The word filled her with horror.

Day after week after month she dogged Narcissus' footsteps. In her unhappiness she grew pale and thin, and when all her beauty had faded because of her love for him, he said, "Oh do go away! I hate the sight of you. Do you really suppose I could ever care for a stick-insect like you? Look at yourself!"

"Look at yourself! . . . Look at yourself!" sobbed Echo.

"Gladly," said the vain young man, and went to the pool in the centre of the forest and examined his reflection.

Echo's love turned to hate, and though she had no words, she wished a wicked, wordless wish. She wished that Narcissus should one day love as she loved him, and suffer for it as she was suffering.

Then she wandered away into the forest where, in her misery, she grew thinner and thinner, paler and paler. At last her body faded away altogether. Only her voice was left to blow about with the leaves.

All this while, Narcissus sat by the pool staring at his reflection. Somehow he could not seem to tear himself away. The more he looked, the more he liked what he saw. Narcissus fell in love with the face in the water, just as Echo had fallen in love with him. He longed to kiss those lips, just as Echo

had longed to kiss his. At last, leaning down towards the shining pool, he kissed the water—and the face reflected there dissolved into ripples.

"Oh don't go!" Narcissus reached out and plunged his hand into the water, but only managed to shatter the reflection altogether. So he sat very still and gazed and gazed and gazed . . .

Meanwhile, in her palace, Hera, queen of the gods, regretted her temper and sent her handmaidens to look for Echo and forgive her. They searched the high rocks and wooded places, but when they called her name—"Echo! Echo!"—their words simply floated back to them on the breeze: " . . . Echo! . . . Echo! . . . Echo!"

They did find one thing, though—a pretty yellow and white flower growing beside a pond. It leaned out over the water as if admiring its own reflection in the pool.

For Narcissus had taken root where he sat. He too had pined away in hopeless love, until all that remained of his body were tissuey petals and a bending stalk.

"I've never seen this kind of flower before," said one of the nymphs. "I wonder what it's called."

And the breeze in the woods seemed to whisper, "Narcissus! Narcissus!"

To this day, the same flower can be found growing wild on the banks of ponds, leaning out over the water as if in love with its own reflection. And people call it narcissus, though they have long since forgotten the vain shepherd boy.

Daedalus and Icarus

The island of Crete was ruled by King Minos, whose reputation for wickedness had spread to every shore. One day he summoned to his country a famous inventor named Daedalus. "Come, Daedalus, and bring your son, Icarus, too. I have a job for you, and I pay well."

King Minos wanted Daedalus to build him a palace, with soaring towers and a high, curving roof. In the cellars there was to be a maze of many corridors—so twisting and dark that any man who once ventured in there would never find his way out again.

"What is it for?" asked Daedalus. "Is it a treasure vault? Is it a prison to hold criminals?"

But Minos only replied, "Build my labyrinth as I told you. I pay you to build, not to ask questions."

So Daedalus held his tongue and set to work. When the palace was finished, he looked at it with pride, for there was nowhere in the world so fine. But when he found out the purpose of the maze in the basement, he shuddered with horror.

For at the heart of that maze, King Minos put a beast—a thing too horrible to describe. He called it the Minotaur, and he fed it on men and women!

Then Daedalus wanted to leave Crete at once, and forget both maze and Minotaur. So he went to King Minos to ask for his money.

"I regret," said King Minos, "I cannot let you leave Crete, Daedalus.

DAEDALUS AND ICARUS

You are the only man who knows the secret of the maze and how to escape from it. The secret must never leave this island. So I'm afraid I must keep you and Icarus here a while longer."

"How much longer?" gasped Daedalus.

"Oh—just until you die," replied Minos cheerfully. "But never mind. I have plenty of work for a man as clever as you."

Daedalus and Icarus lived in great comfort in King Minos' palace. But they lived the life of prisoners. Their rooms were in the tallest palace tower, with beautiful views across the island. They ate delectable food and wore expensive clothes. But at night the door of their fine apartment was locked, and a guard stood outside. It was a comfortable prison, but it was a prison, even so. Daedalus was deeply unhappy.

Every day he put seed out on the window sill, for the birds. He liked to

study their brilliant colours, the clever overlapping of their feathers, the way they soared on the sea wind. It comforted him to think that they at least were free to come and go. The birds had only to spread their wings and they could leave Crete behind them, whereas Daedalus and Icarus must stay for ever in their luxurious cage.

Young Icarus could not understand his father's unhappiness. "But I like it here," he said. "The king gives us gold and this tall tower to live in."

Daedalus groaned. "But to work for such a wicked man, Icarus! And to be prisoners all our days . . . We shan't stay. We shan't!"

"But we can't get away, can we?" said Icarus. "How can anybody escape from an island? Fly?" He snorted with laughter.

Daedalus did not answer. He scratched his head and stared out of the window at the birds pecking seed on the sill.

From that day onwards, he got up early each morning and stood at the open window. When a bird came for the seed, Daedalus begged it to spare him one feather. Then each night, when everyone else had gone to bed, Daedalus worked by candlelight on his greatest invention of all.

Early mornings. Late nights. A whole year went by. Then one morning Icarus was woken by his father shaking his shoulder. "Get up, Icarus, and don't make a sound. We are leaving Crete."

"But how? It's impossible!"

Daedalus pulled out a bundle from under his bed. "I've been making something, Icarus." Inside were four great folded fans of feathers. He stretched them out on the bed. They were wings! "I sewed the feathers together with strands of wool from my blanket. Now hold still."

Daedalus melted down a candle and daubed his son's shoulders with sticky wax. "Yes, I know it's hot, but it will soon cool." While the wax was still soft, he stuck two of the wings to Icarus' shoulder blades.

"Now you must help me put on my wings, Son. When the wax sets hard, you and I will fly away from here, as free as birds!"

"I'm scared!" whispered Icarus as he stood on the narrow window ledge, his knees knocking and his huge wings drooping down behind. The lawns and courtyards of the palace lay far below. The royal guards looked as small as ants. "This won't work!"

"Courage, son!" said Daedalus. "Keep your arms out wide and fly close to me. Above all—are you listening, Icarus?"

"Y-y-yes, Father."

"Above all, don't fly too high! Don't fly too close to the sun!"

"Don't fly too close to the sun," Icarus repeated, with his eyes tight shut. Then he gave a cry as his father nudged him off the window sill.

He plunged downwards. With a crack, the feathers behind him filled with wind, and Icarus found himself flying. Flying!

"*I'm flying!*" he crowed.

The little guards looked up in astonishment, and wagged their swords, and pointed and shouted, "Tell the king! Daedalus and Icarus are . . . are . . . flying away!"

By dipping first one wing, then the other, Icarus found that he could turn to the left and the right. The wind tugged at his hair. His legs trailed out behind him. He saw the fields and streams as he had never seen them before!

Then they were out over the sea. The seagulls pecked at him angrily, so Icarus flew higher, where they could not reach him.

He copied their shrill cry and taunted them: "You can't catch me!"

"Now remember, don't fly too high!" called Daedalus, but his words were drowned by the screaming of the gulls.

"I'm the first boy ever to fly! I'm making history! I shall be famous!" thought Icarus, as he flew up and up, higher and higher.

At last Icarus was looking the sun itself in the face. "Think you're the highest thing in the sky, do you?" he jeered. "I can fly just as high as you! Higher, even!" He did not notice the drops of sweat on his forehead: he was so determined to out-fly the sun.

DAEDALUS AND ICARUS

Soon its vast heat beat on his face and on his back and on the great wings stuck on with wax. The wax softened. The wax trickled. The wax dripped. One feather came unstuck. Then a plume of feathers fluttered slowly down.

Icarus stopped flapping his wings. His father's words came back to him clearly now: *"Don't fly too near to the sun!"*

With a great sucking noise, the wax on his shoulders came unstuck. Icarus tried to catch hold of the wings, but they just folded up in his hands. He plunged down, his two fists full of feathers—down and down and down.

The clouds did not stop his fall.

The seagulls did not catch him in their beaks.

His own father could only watch as Icarus hurtled head first into the glittering sea and sank deep down among the sharks and eels and squid. And all that was left of proud Icarus was a litter of waxy feathers floating on the sea.

Arachne the Spinner

Once, when all cloths and clothes were woven by hand, there was a needlewoman called Arachne more skilful than all the rest. Her tapestries were so lovely that people paid a fortune to buy them. Tailors and weavers came from miles around just to watch Arachne at work on her loom. Her shuttle flew to and fro, and her fingers plucked the strands as if she were making music rather than cloth.

"The gods certainly gave you an amazing talent," said her friends.

"Gods? Bodkins! There's nothing the gods could teach me about weaving. I can weave better than any god or goddess."

Her friends turned rather pale. "Better not let the goddess Athene hear you say that."

"Don't care who hears it. I'm the best there is," said Arachne.

An old lady sitting behind her examined the yarns Arachne had spun that morning, feeling their delightful texture between finger and thumb. "So if there were a competition between you and the goddess Athene, you think you would win?" she said.

"She wouldn't stand a chance," said Arachne. "Not against me."

All of a sudden the old lady's grey hair began to float like smoke about her head and turn to golden light. A swish of wind blew her old coat into shreds and revealed a breastplate of silver and a robe of dazzling white. She grew taller and taller until she stood head and shoulders above the crowd. There was no mistaking the beautiful grey-eyed goddess, Athene.

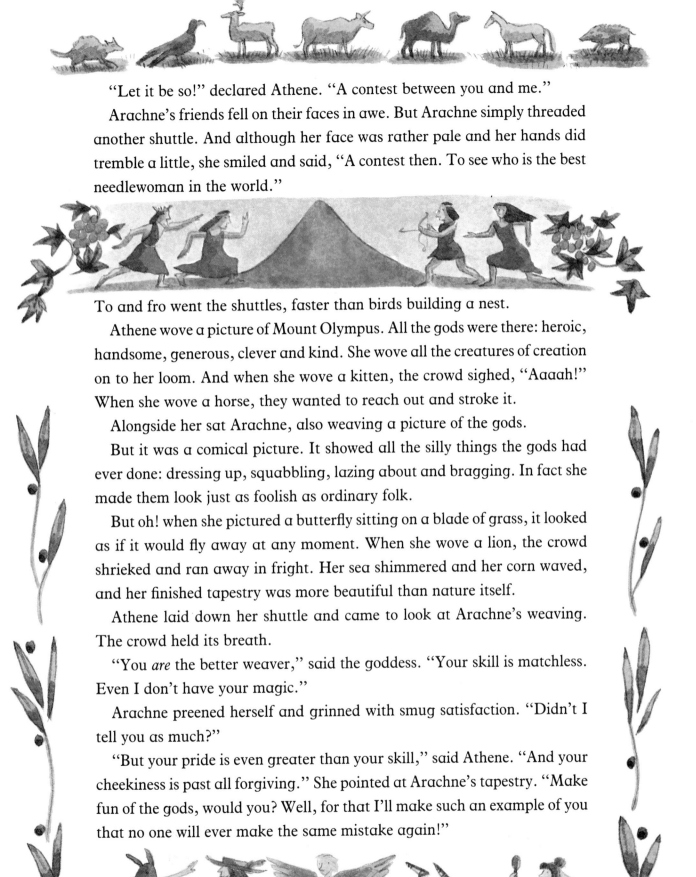

"Let it be so!" declared Athene. "A contest between you and me."

Arachne's friends fell on their faces in awe. But Arachne simply threaded another shuttle. And although her face was rather pale and her hands did tremble a little, she smiled and said, "A contest then. To see who is the best needlewoman in the world."

To and fro went the shuttles, faster than birds building a nest.

Athene wove a picture of Mount Olympus. All the gods were there: heroic, handsome, generous, clever and kind. She wove all the creatures of creation on to her loom. And when she wove a kitten, the crowd sighed, "Aaaah!" When she wove a horse, they wanted to reach out and stroke it.

Alongside her sat Arachne, also weaving a picture of the gods.

But it was a comical picture. It showed all the silly things the gods had ever done: dressing up, squabbling, lazing about and bragging. In fact she made them look just as foolish as ordinary folk.

But oh! when she pictured a butterfly sitting on a blade of grass, it looked as if it would fly away at any moment. When she wove a lion, the crowd shrieked and ran away in fright. Her sea shimmered and her corn waved, and her finished tapestry was more beautiful than nature itself.

Athene laid down her shuttle and came to look at Arachne's weaving. The crowd held its breath.

"You *are* the better weaver," said the goddess. "Your skill is matchless. Even I don't have your magic."

Arachne preened herself and grinned with smug satisfaction. "Didn't I tell you as much?"

"But your pride is even greater than your skill," said Athene. "And your cheekiness is past all forgiving." She pointed at Arachne's tapestry. "Make fun of the gods, would you? Well, for that I'll make such an example of you that no one will ever make the same mistake again!"

She took the shuttle out of Arachne's hands and pushed it into her mouth.
Then, just as Athene had changed from an old woman into her true shape,
she transformed Arachne.

The girl's arms stuck to her sides, and left only her long, clever fingers
straining and scrabbling. Her body shrank down to a black blob no bigger
than an ink blot: an end of thread still curled out of its mouth. Athene used
the thread to hang Arachne up on a tree, and left her dangling there.

"Weave your tapestries for ever!" said the goddess. "And however
wonderful they are, people will only shudder at the sight of them and pull
them to shreds."

*

It all came true. For Arachne had been turned into the first spider, doomed for ever to spin webs in the corners of rooms, in bushes, in dark, unswept places. And though cobwebs are as lovely a piece of weaving as you'll ever see, just look how people hurry to sweep them away.

King Midas

There was once a king called Midas who was almost as stupid as he was greedy.

When there was a music competition between the two gods Pan and Apollo, Midas was asked to be judge. Now Pan was Midas' friend, so instead of listening to the music to judge whose was best, he decided to let Pan win even before they began to play.

Comparing Apollo's music with Pan's is like comparing a golden trumpet with a tin whistle. But Midas had already made up his mind.

"Pan was the better! Oh definitely! No doubt about it. Pan was the better," he said. On and on he went, praising Pan, until Apollo turned quite scarlet with rage and pointed a magic finger at King Midas.

"There is something wrong with your ears if you think Pan's music is better than mine."

"Nothing's wrong with my ears," said foolish King Midas.

"Oh no? Well, we can soon change that!"

When he got home, Midas' ears were itching. He looked in the mirror and—horror of horrors!—his ears were growing. Longer and longer they grew, furrier and furrier, until he had brown and pink donkey's ears.

Midas found he could hide the ears if he crammed them both into a tall hat. "Nobody must see them," he thought as he walked about with his hat pulled down over his eyes. All day he wore it. He even wore it at night, so that the queen would not see his ass's ears.

Nobody noticed. It was a great relief. They only saw that the king wore a tall hat all day long, and hurried to do the same, thinking it was the latest fashion.

But there was one person from whom Midas could not hide his secret. When the barber came to cut his hair, the dreadful truth came out.

The barber gasped. The barber stared. The barber stuffed a towel into his mouth to keep himself from laughing.

"You will tell no one!" commanded King Midas.

"Of course not! Never! No one! I promise!" babbled the barber, and cut the king's hair and helped him back on with his hat. It was to be their secret, never to be told.

The barber had given his promise. He never broke his promises. But oh dear! It was such a hard secret to keep! He ached to tell somebody. He would suddenly burst out laughing in public and could not explain why. He lay awake at nights, for fear of talking in his sleep. He kept that secret until he thought it would burn holes in him! But at last he just had to tell it.

The barber took a very long walk, right away from town, all the way to the river. He dug a hole in the ground and put his head deep down it. Then he whispered into the hole, *"King Midas has long ass's ears!"*

After that, he felt a lot better.

And the rain rained and the grass grew and the reeds by the river grew too.

*

Meanwhile, Midas (wearing his tall cap, of course) was walking in his garden when he met a satyr—half-man, half-horse. The satyr was lost. Midas gave him breakfast and directed him on his way.

"I'm so grateful," said the satyr. "Permit me to reward you. I shall grant you one wish."

He could have wished to be rid of his ass's ears, but no. At once Midas' head filled with pictures of money, wealth, treasure . . . *gold*! His eyes glistened. "Oh please, please! Grant that everything I touch turns to gold!"

"Oof. Not a good idea," said the satyr. "Think again."

But Midas insisted. That was his wish. The satyr shrugged and went on his way.

"Huh! I knew it was too good to be true," said King Midas and he was so disappointed that he picked up a pebble to throw after the satyr.

The stone turned to gold in his palm.

"My wish! The satyr granted it after all!" cried Midas, and did a little dance on the spot. He ran to a tree and touched it. Sure enough, the twigs and branches turned to gold. He ran back to his palace and stroked every wall, chair, table and lamp. They all turned to gold. When he brushed against the curtains, even they turned solid with a sudden clang.

"Prepare me a feast!" Midas commanded. "Being rich makes me hungry!"

The servants ran to fetch meat and bread, fruit and wine, while Midas touched each dish and plate (because it pleased him to eat off gold). When the food arrived, he clutched up a wing of chicken and bit into it.

Clang. It was hard and cold between his lips. The celery scratched his tongue. The bread broke a tooth. Every bite of food turned to gold as he touched it. The wine rattled in its goblet, solid as an egg in an egg cup.

"Don't stand there staring! Fetch me something I can eat!" Midas told a servant, giving him a push . . . But it was a golden statue of a servant that toppled over and fell with a thud.

Just then, the queen came in. "What's this I hear about a wish?" she asked, and went to kiss her husband.

"Don't come near! Don't touch me!" he shrieked, and jumped away from her. But his little son, who was too young to understand, ran and hugged Midas around the knees. "Papa! Papa! Pa—"

Silence. His son was silent. The boy's golden arms were still hooped round Midas' knees. His little golden mouth was open, but no sound came out.

Midas ran to his bedroom and locked the door. But he could not sleep that night, for the pillow turned to gold under his head. He was so hungry, so thirsty, so lonely. So afraid. "Oh you gods! Take away this dreadful wish! I never realised!"

There was a clip-clopping of hoofs and the satyr put his head through the window. "I did try to tell you," he said.

Midas fell on his knees on the golden floor. His golden robe clanged and swung on him like a giant bell. His tall cap fell to the ground like a metal cooking pot. "Take it back! Please ask the gods to take back my wish!" he begged.

"With ears like that, I think you have troubles enough," said the satyr, laughing loudly. "Very well. Go and wash in the river. But do remember not to be so silly another time."

King Midas ran through the long grass, pushed his way through the long reeds, and leapt into the river. The ripples filled with gold dust, but the water itself did not turn to gold. Nor did the river bank as Midas pulled himself out. He was cured!

He carried buckets of water back to the palace and threw them over the little golden statue in the dining room. And there stood his little son, soaked from head to foot and starting to cry.

*

By this time, the grass had grown tall in the fields, and the reeds by the river were taller still. When the wind blew they rustled. When the wind blew harder they murmured. When the wind blew harder still they whispered, *"King Midas has long ass's ears!"*

And on some windy days the reeds sang so loudly that everyone heard them for miles around: *"King Midas has long ass's ears!"*

And that is how King Midas' secret is known to us all today.

Perseus

Long ago, when fortune-tellers told the truth, there lived a very frightened man. Like any father, King Acrisius of Argos loved his daughter, Danaë, and her baby, who was called Perseus. But one day he made the mistake of visiting a fortune-teller.

"You will be killed by Danaë's son," said the fortune-teller to the king.

At once Acrisius gave orders for a wooden chest to be carried to the beach and set down by the water's edge.

"A chest, sire?" said his servants.

"Yes, a chest—with a lid and a big padlock. And hurry!"

Down on the beach, rough soldiers squeezed Danaë into the chest, and tossed her baby in on top of her before slamming shut the lid. As the chest floated out to sea, King Acrisius stood and waved it goodbye. "They're bound to drown," he was thinking. "But I didn't kill them, did I? Nobody can say I killed them."

Instead of sinking, the chest floated. For days it floated across the sea until it was caught in the nets of a young fisherman near the shore of a faraway kingdom.

The fisherman, whose name was Dictys, took Danaë to the little wooden shack where he lived, and showed her and baby Perseus great kindness. Unfortunately, the king of that country was not as good a man as Dictys. King Polydectes liked to collect wives, as other people collect pictures. And as soon as he heard about Danaë, he wanted to add her to his collection.

41

Danaë politely said 'no' when King Polydectes proposed to her. And she went on saying 'no' for seventeen years.

By this time, the king was furious.

"Enough of asking nicely! Guards, go and seize Danaë and fetch her here to be married right away!"

He had forgotten that after seventeen years her son, Perseus, had grown into a fine, strong young man. Perseus beat the guards soundly and sent them back to Polydectes all battered and bruised.

"That Perseus is an amazing young man, sire!" they panted. "He swears his mother shan't marry anyone unless she wants to. He says he'll protect her day and night."

King Polydectes ground his teeth. "I see I must get rid of this wretched boy." So Polydectes challenged Perseus to a dare—the hardest he could imagine.

"I dare you to fetch me the head of the Gorgon Medusa," he said.

Medusa was once a beautiful but vain girl, who had made the mistake of boasting—in the gods' hearing—that no one, not even a goddess, was more beautiful than she. For her punishment, she was changed into a gorgon—a monster with glaring eyes and snakes for hair. Whoever looked at her was turned into stone.

Perseus fell right into the king's trap. "I leave at once!" he cried.

"Bravo!" cheered the courtiers. "Well said, Perseus!"

"Bravo!" thought King Polydectes. "He'll die, of course."

"Bravo!" cried the gods, looking down from Mount Olympus. "What a brave boy that Perseus is. He deserves our help."

"I'll lend him my feathered shoes," said Hermes.

"I'll lend him my bright shield," said the goddess Athene.

"I'll lend him my helmet of invisibility," said Pluto, "and a thick bag to put Medusa's head in."

"I shall watch, but not help," said Zeus. "Perseus must match his brave words with brave deeds."

A few days later, having kissed his mother, Danaë, goodbye, Perseus set off. He was carrying nothing more than a sword, but soon he came across a helmet lying in the road. He pulled it on, thinking it might be useful if he had to fight a monster. He stared down at his feet. But they had disappeared. He had no feet! Nor hands! Nor clothes, nor body! Even the helmet itself was invisible when Perseus had it on his head.

Perseus went a little further and found a shield lying in the road. Its metal was polished mirror-bright. He slung the shield over his back, thinking it might be useful if he had to fight a monster, and continued on his way.

A little further on, he found a pair of winged sandals. He buckled them on and—"Wo-wo-woah!"—found himself walking on air! Up, up, up and over the treetops the flying shoes carried him. Such sandals could not fail to be useful if he had to fight a monster. He looked up to heaven and thanked the gods for their presents, before continuing on his way to look for Medusa.

But to find her, Perseus knew he had first to find the three Grey Sisters. They alone knew where the gruesome Gorgon Medusa had her lair. These three revolting old women lived on a rocky clifftop, and kept watch for passers-by to cook in their iron cauldron. They could not all keep watch at once, though. Between the three of them, they had only one grey eye.

When he was still a long way from their den, Perseus pulled on the helmet of invisibility. As he got closer, he could hear the grisly sisters quarrelling about their supper. They could not decide whose turn it was to eat. Between the three of them, they had only one rotten tooth.

Then one ugly sister shrieked, "My turn for the eye!"

The user of the eye sighed, and took it out of her head: "Here you are then."

"Where? Put it in my hand, why don't you?"

"I have done. Don't tell me you've dropped it."

"You never gave it me! Don't go blaming me!"

Arguing furiously, they scrabbled about, feeling for the one lost grey eye.

"I have what you are looking for," said invisible Perseus.

The Grey Sisters set up a terrible wailing. "Who's that? Tear him to pieces, sisters! He's stolen our precious eye!"

"Calm yourselves, ladies," said Perseus politely. "I'll give you back your eye . . . "

"Good boy! Here! Give! Give! What are you waiting for!"

" . . . as soon as you tell me how to find the Gorgon Medusa."

"Never! No! It's a secret!"

"Can't tell!"

"Won't tell!"

"Oh, so I can toss this eye of yours into that cauldron, can I? Or let it roll away down the mountainside?"

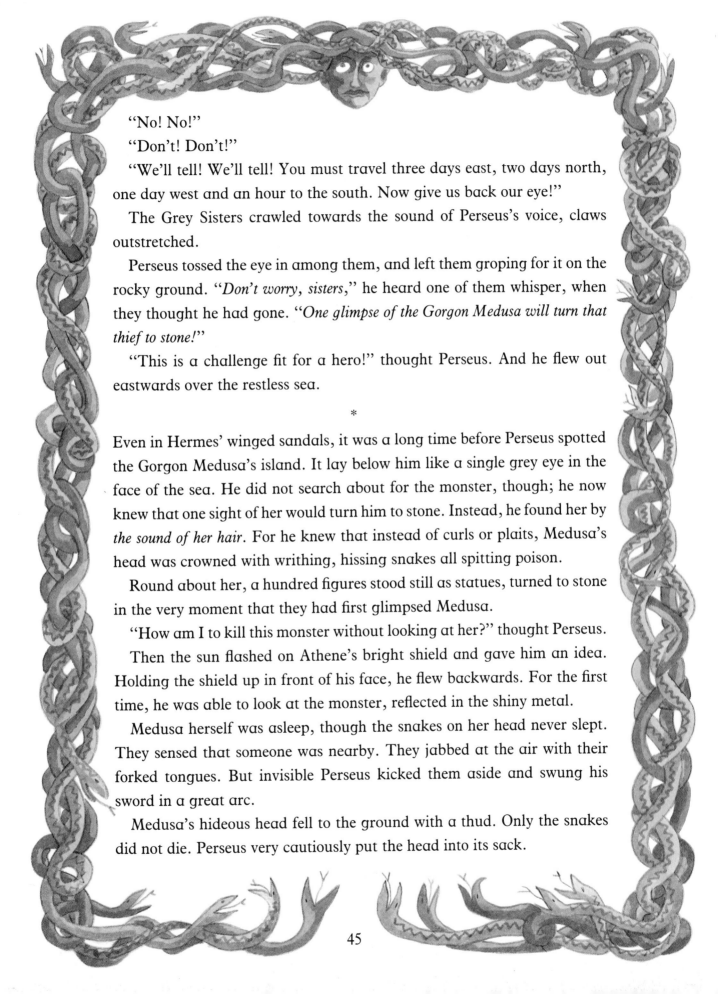

"No! No!"

"Don't! Don't!"

"We'll tell! We'll tell! You must travel three days east, two days north, one day west and an hour to the south. Now give us back our eye!"

The Grey Sisters crawled towards the sound of Perseus's voice, claws outstretched.

Perseus tossed the eye in among them, and left them groping for it on the rocky ground. "*Don't worry, sisters,*" he heard one of them whisper, when they thought he had gone. "*One glimpse of the Gorgon Medusa will turn that thief to stone!*"

"This is a challenge fit for a hero!" thought Perseus. And he flew out eastwards over the restless sea.

*

Even in Hermes' winged sandals, it was a long time before Perseus spotted the Gorgon Medusa's island. It lay below him like a single grey eye in the face of the sea. He did not search about for the monster, though; he now knew that one sight of her would turn him to stone. Instead, he found her by *the sound of her hair.* For he knew that instead of curls or plaits, Medusa's head was crowned with writhing, hissing snakes all spitting poison.

Round about her, a hundred figures stood still as statues, turned to stone in the very moment that they had first glimpsed Medusa.

"How am I to kill this monster without looking at her?" thought Perseus.

Then the sun flashed on Athene's bright shield and gave him an idea. Holding the shield up in front of his face, he flew backwards. For the first time, he was able to look at the monster, reflected in the shiny metal.

Medusa herself was asleep, though the snakes on her head never slept. They sensed that someone was nearby. They jabbed at the air with their forked tongues. But invisible Perseus kicked them aside and swung his sword in a great arc.

Medusa's hideous head fell to the ground with a thud. Only the snakes did not die. Perseus very cautiously put the head into its sack.

On the way back, as he flew over a parched desert, the Gorgon's blood dripped through the sack on to the sand below. As each drop touched the ground, a serpent wriggled away and burrowed into the sand.

*

As he flew homewards, Perseus passed over a country troubled by a terrible monster. It was a sea serpent which devoured swimmers, snatched fishermen off the beach, and even dragged itself ashore to grab people off the town streets and carry them out to sea.

"What shall we do?" wailed the king. "How can I rid my country of this terrible danger?"

His fortune-teller said, "The gods are angry. There is only one thing you can do. You must sacrifice your most precious possession to the sea monster. You must feed it your own daughter, Andromeda." The king howled and tore his hair, but the fortune-teller insisted: Andromeda must die.

As the guards dragged Andromeda down to the seashore, she caught sight of a handsome young friend of hers. "Phineas! Oh, Phineas, help me! I was to be your bride. Surely you won't let them do this? Save me!"

But Phineas turned away his eyes. "They say nothing else will work. Do you want us all to be eaten in our beds, you selfish girl? You ought to be proud to do this for your country." And he hurried away with his fingers in his ears.

So Andromeda was chained to a ledge on the cliff and left as a sacrifice to the sea serpent. She looked out to sea. Was that a giant fin cutting through the waves? Was that a huge tail beating the sea into a black foam? Andromeda pulled at her chains and screamed with all her might.

All that Perseus heard, as he flew overhead, was a small, piping cry, like a seagull's call. But it was enough to make him look down. He saw the monster speeding through the water: he saw the girl chained against the cliff.

Like a hawk, Perseus swooped out of the sky. But the serpent reared up out of the water and tossed him against the cliff. Perseus' shield fell from his shoulder, the helmet and bag fell from his grasp. He drew his sword and leapt between the princess and the monster's open mouth, and drove his sword into the beast's shoulder. Snaking its neck with pain, it lashed at him with its tail and knocked him into the sea. To keep from drowning, Perseus clung to the only thing he could—the monster's slimy neck. Time and again he plunged in his sword. The beast writhed once, twice, three times . . . then rolled over on to its back, quite dead.

When Perseus pulled himself wearily out of the water, Andromeda looked down at him with eyes full of thanks. High above, on the clifftops, the people of the country began to cheer and clap.

The news was rushed to the king, who sent for Perseus at once. "Ask any reward, young man, and you shall have it. You have saved our one and only daughter!"

"What else could I do?" said Perseus shyly. "She is so beautiful. The best reward I could ever think of is to have Andromeda for my wife."

The wedding had just begun when Phineas arrived. He raged into the palace with an army of fifty men. "Where is he, this thief with the feathery boots? How dare he steal the girl promised to me in marriage!"

"But, Phineas! You were quite happy for me to be eaten by the sea monster!" said Andromeda. "Perseus risked his life to save mine."

"Then he won't mind dying now, will he?" sneered Phineas.

Fifty men closed in on Perseus. Each one carried a spear: each raised his arm to throw it. How could Perseus fend off fifty spears with a single sword? In the corner of the room lay the black bag. Perseus dived towards it, loosened the cords, and plunged in his hand. "*All those who love Perseus, shut your eyes!*" he cried, and dragged out the Gorgon Medusa's head.

Fifty spears clattered to the floor, dropped by hands that had turned to stone. His attackers stood about like ugly statues, doomed to stand for ever with one arm lifted. Perseus quickly returned the head to its bag, for fear Andromeda should open her eyes.

Next day, with Medusa's head safely covered up and stowed away on board, bride and groom set sail for home.

With Perseus out of the way, King Polydectes thought he could force Danaë to marry him. "Make ready for your wedding!" he commanded her. "I've wasted enough time!"

Danaë was panic-stricken. Dictys, the kind fisherman, tried to protect her, but soon five hundred soldiers surrounded Danaë and her friend.

"I've waited long enough!" declared King Polydectes. "Today shall be your wedding day, Danaë! Look. Here are five hundred ushers to bring you to the temple!" The soldiers drew their swords.

Suddenly a murmur ran through the ranks, as two people came pushing towards the king: a young man and a girl.

"I've brought you the Gorgon Medusa's head, your majesty," said Perseus. "But I see the challenge was only an excuse to get me out of the way."

King Polydectes held his sides and roared with laughter.

"Brought me the Gorgon Medusa's head? You lying little brat! Nobody could do that! Well, who cares what you really have in that sack? I'm going to marry your mother, whether you like it or not, so you may as well enjoy the wedding!"

"You don't believe me?" asked Perseus. "Then see for yourself. See your wedding present!" Once more he reached into the sack. Andromeda covered her eyes. Perseus turned aside his head. But Polydectes and his soldiers all stared at the thing in his hand. They stared and stared, and are staring still, still standing as they stood in that moment when the Gorgon Medusa's head turned them all to stone.

When it was all over, Perseus flew far out to sea and sank the monster's head in deep water, where it turned all the seaweed to shining coral. Then he left the magic weapons out under the evening sky, and next day they were gone.

Dictys became king in place of the wicked Polydectes, and there were great festivities because everybody liked the old fisherman. Danaë married him, and was happy at last. All the kings, queens, princes and princesses of the world gathered for the wedding and to watch a festive day of sports. There was running, jumping, wrestling, throwing the javelin . . . Perseus himself put his name down for the discus-throwing contest.

When it came to his turn, he threw the brass discus much higher and harder and further than any other competitor. But the wind caught it and spun it into the watching crowd. There was an awful silence. An old man had been hit! He was dead.

"Who is he? Doesn't anybody know?" asked Perseus, tearing at his hair with anguish.

"It is your grandfather," said Danaë gently. "Poor man. It was his fate that you should kill him. Don't blame yourself. Nobody can cheat Fate. Do you realise what this means? Now you have a kingdom of your own! Now you are King Perseus!"

But Perseus would not rule over Acrisius' kingdom. He was too sad at having killed his own grandfather. Instead he travelled with Andromeda to an empty land and began a new kingdom there, the noblest kingdom in all the world.

The Twelve Labours of Heracles

There was once a baby born who was so remarkable that the gods themselves stared down at his cradle. He was called Heracles, and when huge snakes slithered into his crib to strangle him, he knotted and plaited them as if they were pieces of string, and threw them out again.

For Heracles was strong—fantastically strong—stronger than you and me and a hundred others put together. Fortunately, he was also gentle and kind, so that his friends had nothing to fear from him. His schoolteacher made him promise never to touch alcoholic drink, though. "If you were ever to get drunk, Heracles," the schoolmaster said, "who knows what terrible thing you might do with that great strength of yours!"

Heracles promised, and he truly meant to keep his promise. But then his friends all drank at parties, his family always had wine with their meals: it seemed foolish for Heracles to ask for fruit juice or water. So he was tempted to take just one glass of wine—and after that another—and another—and another. Soon he was roaring drunk, throwing punches in all directions. When the wine's work was done, Heracles' own family lay dead on the floor, and Heracles was an outcast hated by everyone and most of all by himself.

For his crime, he was condemned to serve King Eurystheus as a slave for seven years. Eurystheus was a mean, spiteful man—whose kingdom was overrun by a great many problems—and he decided to set Heracles the twelve most dangerous tasks he could think of—tasks that were to become known as the Twelve Labours of Heracles.

A giant lion was terrorising his kingdom, eating men, women and children. "Go and kill the lion, slave," he told Heracles.

Heracles was so miserable that he did not much care whether he lived or died. He found the lion's den and strode in, with no weapon but his bare hands. When the beast sprang at him, Heracles took it by the throat and shook it like a rug, then wrung it out like washing. When it was dead, he skinned it and wore the lion skin for a tunic, knotting the paws around his waist and shoulders.

If King Eurystheus was grateful, he did not show it, but simply set Heracles his Second Labour. "If you can kill lions," he said, "you may as well try to kill the Hydra."

The Hydra was a water serpent which lived in the middle of a swamp. When it was born, it had nine heads. But each time one was cut off, two new heads grew to replace it. By the time Heracles came face to face with the Hydra, it had fifty heads, all gnashing their horrible teeth.

THE TWELVE LABOURS OF HERACLES

Heracles was quick with his sword and nimble on his feet. But though he slashed through many snaking necks without being bitten, the struggle only became more difficult. The heads just multiplied! So Heracles ran off a short way and lit a fire. Then he heated his wooden club red-hot and, with his sword in one hand and his club in the other, he re-entered the fight.

This time, as he cut through each neck, he singed the ragged end with his red-hot club, and the head did not regrow. At last the Hydra looked like nothing more than a knobbly tree stump.

There was no time to rest after fighting the Hydra. King Eurystheus sent him to capture a stag with golden antlers, then to kill a huge wild boar.

Heracles' Fifth Labour was a particularly unpleasant one: to clean the Augean stables.

Lord Augeas kept one thousand animals penned up in sties and stables stretching the length of a foul valley. He was too idle to clean out his animals and too mean to hire farmhands. So the wretched beasts stood up to their bellies in dung. People for miles around complained about the smell.

Heracles stood on a hilltop, looking down on the valley, holding his nose. He saw a river bubbling close by, and it gave him an idea. Moving boulders as easily as if they were feather pillows, he built a dam, so that the river flowed out of its course and down the valley instead. Startled horses and cows and goats and sheep staggered in a torrent of rushing water, but the dung beneath them was scoured away by the river. Heracles only had to demolish the dam with one blow of his club, and the river flowed back to its old river bed. The animals stood shivering and shaking themselves dry, in a green, clean valley.

King Eurystheus was ready and waiting with his next three commands. Heracles was to destroy a flock of bloodthirsty man-eating birds, tame the mad bull of Crete, and capture the famous wild horses which could run faster than the wind.

By now the king had begun to feel very nervous of his slave. He had a big bronze vase made and hid inside it whenever Heracles came back from doing his work.

"The mad bull is tamed, master. The man-eating birds are dead, and your wild horses are outside in the yard," said Heracles, when he returned soon after. "What must I do next?"

But Eurystheus was running out of problems and his mind turned to thoughts of getting rich with the help of Heracles.

"Get me the jewelled belt worn by the Queen of the Amazons!" said the king, from inside his urn.

Here was one task for which Heracles did not mean to use his great strength. He simply went to the queen of those savage female warriors and explained why he was there. She took an instant liking to him and gave him the belt straight away. Unfortunately, word spread through the camp that Heracles had come to kill the queen and he had to fight a thousand angry women, fierce as wasps, before he could escape with the jewelled belt.

And so it continued. No sooner did Heracles finish one task, than he was set another one. To fetch King Eurystheus the legendary giant oxen, Heracles made a bridge over the sea by bending two mountain peaks out across the water. To fetch Pluto's three-headed dog, Cerberus, he travelled down to the fearful Underworld.

But the twelfth and last and greediest of the king's commands was for Heracles to bring him the apples of the Hesperides. These magical fruit grew on a tree in a garden at the end of the world, and around that tree coiled a dragon which never slept.

Even Heracles, with all his courage and strength, quailed at the thought of fighting the dragon. Better by far that a friend should ask it for the fruit and be allowed to take them. So Heracles went to see a giant named Atlas.

Now Atlas was no ordinary giant, as big as a house. Atlas was the biggest man in the world, and towered above houses, trees, cliffs and hills. He was so tall that the gods had given him the task of holding up the sky and keeping the stars from falling. The sun scorched his neck and the new moon shaved his beard. And for thousands of years he had stood in the one spot.

"How can I go to the end of the world?" said Atlas, when Heracles asked him for the favour. "How can I go *anywhere*?"

"I could hold the sky for you while you were gone," suggested Heracles.

"Could you? Would you? Then I'll do it!" said Atlas.

So Heracles took the sky on his back—though it was the heaviest burden he had ever carried. Atlas stretched himself, then strode away towards the end of the world: the gardeners were members of his family.

Fetching the apples was no hardship. But as the giant hurried back across the world, carrying the precious fruit, he thought how wonderful it felt to be free! As he got closer to home, the thought of carrying that weight of sky again seemed less and less attractive. His steps slowed. When at last he reached Heracles—poor exhausted, bone-bent Heracles—Atlas exclaimed, "I've decided! I'm going to let *you* go on holding up the sky, and I'll deliver these apples to King Eurystheus."

There was a silence. Then Heracles grunted, "Fine. Thank you. It's a great honour to be allowed to hold up heaven. But if you could just help me get a pad across my shoulders before you go . . . these stars do prickle . . . "

So Atlas took charge of the sky again—just while Heracles made a pad for his shoulders. He even gave Heracles the apples to hold, because he needed both hands.

"Well, I'll be on my way now," said Heracles, juggling with the apples as he scurried away. "Most grateful for your help. Perhaps next time, *you*'ll get the better of *me*."

After seven years, Heracles' hard labours came to an end, and he was free. But he was never free from his sorrow at taking that first glass of wine: not until the day he died.

Being only a man and not a god, he did die. But the gods did not forget him. They cut him out in stars and hung him in the sky, to rest from his labours for all time, among the singing planets.

Apollo and Daphne

There was one god who was younger than all the others. Cupid was no more than a boy, but for all that, he was trusted to look after the most important thing of all: falling in love. With his bow and arrows he could shoot straight into the heart of any man or woman. And once his arrow struck, there was no cure for the wound.

One day, when Apollo the sun god saw Cupid with his tiny bow and arrow, he laughed rudely and said, "What's a baby doing carrying the weapons of a warrior? You should leave archery to grown-ups like me!"

Cupid was so angry that he took a gold-tipped arrow from his quiver and shot it, point blank, into Apollo's chest. The sun god felt no pain—well, only a pang. "Ha! Is that the best you can do?" he jeered at Cupid.

Apollo thought he knew all about love. Women were always falling in love with him because he was so handsome. But only when Cupid's golden arrow pierced him did he find out how it felt to be in love himself. His eye came to rest on Daphne—a water nymph, daughter of the River Peleus. And all at once she was Daphne his passion, his dearest darling, his one desire.

Then Cupid fired a second arrow—tipped this time with lead. It pierced Daphne's breast and filled her heart—not with love—but with loathing. From that moment, she hated all men.

"Daphne, I love you!" declared Apollo—but Daphne took to her heels and ran. Through the woods she ran, across the meadows and mountains.

"Come back, Daphne! Where are you going? Why are you running away? I love you! I only want to kiss you and hold you close and tell you how much I love you!"

"Leave me alone!" cried Daphne. "I don't want your love! I don't want your kisses! Stop following me!"

She was fast, but Apollo was faster. He began to catch up with her, so that when he reached out he could feel her hair brush the tips of his fingers. "Don't be afraid! I wouldn't hurt you, would I, loving you the way I do?" The harder she ran, the more he wanted to catch her.

Down ran Daphne to the brink of the river. "Oh, Father River! Help me, please! He has hold of me by my hair! Save me! Save me from Apollo!"

When the river saw how afraid she was, he took pity on her.

"Got you!" cried Apollo triumphantly, catching hold of both her arms.

But suddenly his hands were full of splinters. Ahead of him, Daphne stopped so suddenly that he bloodied his nose and scraped his shins against bark. For Daphne's brown feet had slipped into the soil and taken root, and her arms had turned to branches and her tears to falling leaves. The river had turned her into a green bay tree, and there she stood, trembling, but only because of the breeze.

"I wanted you for my own!" cried Apollo. "If I can't have you as a woman, I'll have you as you are. From today onwards, I declare that the bay tree is sacred to me, the god Apollo. Let every victorious hero returning from the wars, every emperor and king be crowned with a wreath of bay leaves, because Apollo's first love was the green bay tree."

Then he brushed the leaves out of his hair and looked about him for a more friendly woman—one who would smile at him rather than run away.

Theseus and the Minotaur

There used to be a great many kings in the world, because every city and island called itself a kingdom. But one king and one island struck fear into all the rest. King Minos of Crete so terrified his neighbours that they paid him tributes every year to be left in peace. It was King Minos who built a palace with a cellar like a maze. It was King Minos who kept a monster called the Minotaur in this famous Labyrinth and fed it on human flesh.

*

"Why do we send tributes to Crete every year?" Prince Theseus asked his father, the King of Athens.

"To keep King Minos from sinking our ships or making war on us," said King Aegeus (though he did not like to talk about it).

"And what do we send?"

"Seven men and seven women," said the king.

"As slaves?"

"Not as slaves," said the king reluctantly. "To feed the Minotaur."

"How revolting! Never again!" Theseus vowed. "This year *I'll* go as one of the fourteen, and kill this Minotaur!"

Nothing the king could say would change his mind. As the tribute-ship set sail, the old man called from the dockside, "Good luck, Son! I shall keep watch on the clifftop every day. If you succeed, raise a new white sail. If you fail, raise this black one."

"I shall succeed!" called Theseus.

THESEUS AND THE MINOTAUR

King Minos laughed to see the prisoners arrive from Athens. "Who'll be first into the Minotaur's den?" he asked.

"I shall," said Theseus, stepping forward. "I, Prince Theseus of Athens, claim that honour!"

"You boasting young puppy," snarled Minos. "My Minotaur will make short work of *you*. Guards! Put the prince into the Labyrinth!"

Behind the throne, the king's plain little daughter, Ariadne, sat listening. She was ashamed of her father's cruelty, and hated to see how he fed the horrible beast in the basement. She was still more unhappy when she saw brave and handsome Theseus dragged away to feed the monster.

Down went Theseus, into the dark, but he paused, not knowing which way to go. The guards marched away.

"Prince Theseus!"

It was Ariadne. "Here. Take this." She dropped down to him a ball of string. "Even if you can kill the Minotaur, you won't ever find your way back to the entrance unless you use this."

"Excellent!" exclaimed Theseus. "I could marry a girl as clever as you!"
Then he tied one end to the entrance and set off, unwinding the string as he
went, forgetting everything but the Minotaur.

But Ariadne did not forget.

Theseus felt his way in the dark. It was true: without the string he would
soon have been hopelessly lost in the maze of winding corridors. Suddenly,
his fingers brushed warm, wiry hair, then the bony curve of a horn. The
Minotaur bellowed in his ear and flung him through the darkness. It
stamped on him with sharp hoofs. The string was knocked out of his hand.

They fought in utter darkness. The monster, half-man, half-bull, crushed
him between hairy arms and lashed him with its tail. But Theseus took hold
of the horns and twisted them first one way, then the other. He kicked and
butted and struggled, and at last the beast gave a gurgling gasp and fell
dead.

Filled with panic, the prince scrabbled around for the ball of string.
There! No, that was the Minotaur's ear. There! Yes! Now he had only to
wind it in and so retrace his steps.

THESEUS AND THE MINOTAUR

At the door of the Labyrinth, Ariadne stood waiting.

"You're alive! You escaped!" she cried, and she took him by the hand and hurried him away.

They freed the other thirteen prisoners, then ran to the harbour. "You must take me with you, or my father will kill me too!" said the princess.

"Of course! Come aboard!" said Theseus, raising the old black sail with two pulls of his strong arms. The sail filled, and they were at sea before anyone knew they had escaped.

Theseus sat on deck in the sunshine and thought about what he had done. He was proud. His father would be proud, too. "I must change this sail for a white one," he was thinking.

Just then, Ariadne came and sat at his feet, gazing up at him. "How wonderful!" she sighed. "To be free of my wicked father and to be married to a brave prince!"

"Married?" said Theseus, turning rather pale. He suddenly realised that just because Ariadne had saved his life, she expected to marry him! He studied her face. That nose was *very* big. And those eyebrows were *very* thick. "Mmmm," he said. "How wonderful."

On the way home, the ship put in at an island for supplies. Theseus sent Ariadne ashore to buy wine and bread. While she was gone, he set sail and hurried away, breathing a sigh of relief.

"When *I* marry," he thought, "it will be to a beautiful queen or a goddess." He was in such a hurry to get away that he quite forgot to change the black sail for a white one.

King Aegeus, watching day after day from the cliff below Athens, saw the ship as it hove into view. He saw the black sail full of wind. And in that moment, he believed that his son Theseus had been killed and eaten by the Minotaur. He threw himself off the high white cliff into the water below.

And ever afterwards the sea was called the Aegean Sea, after the father of that ungrateful hero, Theseus.

Jason and the Golden Fleece

It's sad, but sometimes brothers hate each other. Pelias hated his older brother, Aeson, because Aeson was the King of Thebes. "*I* want to be king," said Pelias, and took the throne from his brother and put him in prison. But Aeson had a son, and after many years that son came back to fight for his father's rights. His name was Jason.

When Pelias heard that Jason had arrived, he did not send assassins to kill him. He challenged him to a dare. "I'll give up the crown without a fight, if you can prove you are worthy to take it from me. I dare you to go and find the famous Golden Fleece. If you can bring it to me, the crown goes back to your father."

"I accept! I'll do it!" said Jason.

Then Pelias smiled a wicked smile. For he knew that many had tried to take the fiercely-guarded Golden Fleece belonging to King Aeëtes—but none had lived to tell the tale.

*

Jason's first task was to search out the finest shipbuilder in the land.

"Build me a ship finer than any that ever sailed the seas. I'm going in search of the Golden Fleece!"

"But they say the Fleece is guarded by a dragon that never sleeps!" whispered the shipbuilder.

"Then I must put that dragon to sleep for ever!" cried Jason.

He called his ship *Argo*, which means swift, and he mustered a crew from all the heroes of the world and called them his Argonauts. But when he climbed aboard, he did not even know where to start looking for the Golden Fleece. Resting his hand on the wooden figurehead—carved from a magical oak tree—he could feel a throb, like a heartbeat. Suddenly the figurehead turned, and the carved eyes opened, and the carved mouth spoke: "King Phineas will tell you where. Ask poor, poor Phineas!"

Phineas was old and blind. He had chests full of robes and larders full of food. But when Jason and the Argonauts visited him he was as thin as a twig and his clothes hung in rags.

Servants brought delicious food. But no sooner was the table set than in through the windows swooped a flock of hideous birds, their claws snatching, their wings clacking. They had women's heads, with flying hair and munching mouths, and they stole the supper out of the very hands of the Argonauts and slashed at their faces.

"The Harpies! Shelter under the table, sirs!" cried King Phineas. "You'll be safer there."

But Jason drew his sword and cried, "Up, men, and fight!"

He and his crew fought the Harpies until feathers and hair fell like snow. The creatures beat at Jason with their leathery wings, but he cut them out of the air with his sword and jumped on them with his two feet. At last the Harpies fled shrieking across the rooftops and out to sea, never to return.

Jason filled a plate with food and set it in front of the king. "Eat, friend, then tell us how to find the Golden Fleece."

"Don't try it!" begged Phineas. "The Fleece hangs in the Land of Colchis, beyond the Clashing Cliffs. Think of that and tremble!"

"Tremble? I, tremble? Ha!" said Jason grandly. And he gathered his men together and the *Argo* set sail for the Clashing Cliffs.

But the cliffs were a terrifying sight. Two walls of rock, on either side of a narrow strait, crashed together like cymbals. Fire streamed down and sparks flew up, while boulders plunged into the churning sea below.

"We shall be ground to dust!" cried the Argonauts.

"No! Watch the seagulls, men!" cried Jason. "They know when the way ahead is safe. Lean on your oars, and follow the gulls!"

And between one clash of cliffs and the next, the *Argo* sped through, swift as the darting seagulls. Soon they had reached Colchis, Land of the Golden Fleece.

The next day Jason presented himself to the king of the island and told him his story. "I must have the Golden Fleece—it's my destiny," he said.

The king's lip curled. "Well, of course *I* shall let you take my Golden Fleece . . . but the soldiers who guard it might try to stop you. Ha ha!"

Out of his deep purple pockets he pulled handfuls of sharp white teeth. Dragon's teeth! He tossed them in among the Argonauts. As each tooth touched the ground, a warrior sprang up, bristling with weapons. Soon these soldiers outnumbered Jason's men a hundred to one.

"We fought the Harpies, didn't we?" cried Jason to his men. "Surely we can knock out a mouthful of teeth!"

"Kill them!" the king raged at his dragon-tooth army. But soon there was no army left to hear him. The Argonauts had wiped it out. Now nothing stood between Jason and the Golden Fleece.

Except the dragon.

The Fleece hung in a lovely garden. By the gate of the garden stood a woman—the king's daughter. "I watched you fight the dragon-tooth warriors," said Princess Medea to Jason. "You are a true hero, I can see that. But you'll need my magic if you are going to win the Golden Fleece. Marry me and I'll help you."

"You're so beautiful that I'll willingly marry you," said Jason. "But I must lift down the prize by my own strength or I would be cheating."

He set out through flowery groves, across streams, past bushes hung with blossom. But here and there he passed piles of bones. Other heroes had entered the garden before him . . . and met the dragon.

At last Jason found the prize he had come for. The Golden Fleece rested over the branch of a tree—as thick and heavy as a carpet, glistening with golden curls, soft, soft, soft. And round the tree coiled the dragon set to guard it. The monster had no eyelids, it had no name and it had no pity. It looked at Jason with eyes scorched red by sunshine and moonlight. Then it pounced on him with gaping jaws.

Jason drew his sword, but its blade shattered like glass against the dragon's scales. Teeth tore his clothes and fiery breath scorched his hair. Up into the tree he clambered to escape. And when the dragon opened its mouth to lick him down, Jason plunged in his broken sword. The beast gave a terrible roar. Smoke billowed round Jason. Again and again he stabbed, until black smoke dirtied all the king's garden.

The Argonauts, watching from the shore, saw the smoke gather in the sky.

"Where's Jason? Why doesn't he come?" they cried.

Then the sun glinted on a splash of gold—a sheep's fleece. It was draped over Jason's shoulder as he came running down the beach. Alongside him ran a woman as beautiful as the Fleece.

"Aboard, men!" cried Jason. "I've stolen the king's Golden Fleece and his daughter!"

*

So Jason and Princess Medea returned to Thebes—much to the amazement and fury of Pelias. Jason's father, Aeson, was freed from prison, but he refused to put on the crown of Thebes again.

"I'm too tired to rule, Son," he said. "You must be king in my place."

But Medea said gently, "Trust me, father-in-law. I have magic to make you strong and young again."

She poured him a peculiar potion, which sent Aeson to sleep for three days. When he awoke, he had the body of a young man and the wisdom of an old one—and all the energy he needed to rule Thebes.

When wicked old Pelias saw this amazing transformation, he went to Medea and offered her all his money if she would do the same for him. "Make me young again, Medea," he said. "I'd give anything for that!"

So Medea gave him a potion, too, and he fell asleep for three days. Three months. Three years. In fact he never woke up again, because Medea had put him to sleep for ever.

So Jason and Medea lived together as man and wife, and although Jason dressed in simple clothes, his cloak was lined with a golden fleece.

Orpheus and Eurydice

There were once a man and wife so much in love that they wanted nothing but each other. Her name was Eurydice and his was Orpheus. Orpheus was a musician.

Oh, and what a musician! He played a lyre and he sang such songs that the grass at his feet curled with pleasure. Snarling wild animals purred and waved their tails. The trees swayed towards him, tilting their leaves like ears.

Then one day a snake stung Eurydice. She gave a cry of pain and fell to her knees. Orpheus caught her in his arms. "Eurydice! What's the matter!" he cried.

But she could not answer. She was dead. Orpheus was left holding her body, but her soul slipped out of his grasp and sank into the dry, cracked ground—down into the Underworld.

Then Orpheus stopped singing and laid down his lyre. "There is no life without Eurydice," he said. "I must fetch her back."

His friends gasped with horror at such an idea. But Orpheus turned his back on them and travelled down, through the valleys, pits and tunnels of the world, to the shores of the River Styx.

At the river bank Orpheus called out, "Ferryman! Ferryman! Come and row me over, for my wife has come to the Underworld too early, and I must fetch her back home."

There was a splash of oars and a black boat appeared out of the mists.

"Young man, are you mad? No one but the Dead may cross this river and

71

enter the Underworld! Even if I did row you over, you couldn't get past Cerberus who guards the gate!"

"I must," said Orpheus, and the ferryman was so struck by the grief in the young man's face that he let him step aboard.

As the boat glided across the river, a dark shape loomed up, then a terrible barking split the air. It was Cerberus, the three-headed guard dog. Orpheus took his lyre on to his lap and began to play. He played a song without words, and the ferryman stopped splashing his oars to listen. The barking sank to a yelp, then to a whimper. When the boat touched shore, Orpheus stepped out of the boat, still playing.

Throughout the Underworld, the souls of the Dead stopped to listen. Pluto, King of the Dead, also listened. "What's that noise, wife?"

His wife, Persephone, knew at once. "It must be Orpheus the musician! Oh, if he is dead and his spirit ours to keep, we shall have better music here than on earth!"

"Never! Music is forbidden here!" exclaimed Pluto.

At the sight of Orpheus—a man still wearing his earthly body—Pluto jumped up and pointed an angry finger. "You'll be sorry you dared to sneak down here, young man!"

Orpheus simply began to sing. He sang of Eurydice's beauty. He sang of their love. He sang of the spiteful snake and of his unbearable loneliness. When the song finished, Pluto sank back in his throne, his hands over his face, and tears running down into his beard.

"Every time someone dies, there are people who want them alive again," said Pluto. "But you are the only one who ever made me allow this to happen. Eurydice shall return to the earth."

He clapped his hands, and feet could be heard running down a long corridor: the footsteps of Eurydice. Orpheus peered through the gloom for a first glimpse of her dear face.

"If—" said Pluto.

"If?"

"If you can climb back to the sunlight without once turning to look at her face." He laughed unkindly.

Back Orpheus went towards the River Styx, and the swish of a woman's

robes followed him. But he did not look back. Again Orpheus began to play. Again the great dog Cerberus lolled with delight and let him pass, licking him with three tongues. But Orpheus did not look back. Into the rowing boat he stepped, and someone stepped in behind him. The ferryman rowed two passengers across the river.

One last long climb and they would be free of the Underworld! Then Orpheus would be able to take Eurydice in his arms and kiss her and laugh about the dreary Kingdom of the Dead. "Not long now!" he called to her.

Why did Eurydice not reply? Perhaps Pluto had tricked him. Perhaps it was someone else following him. Or perhaps Eurydice had changed during her time in the Underworld, and didn't love her husband any more! Just as the first rays of sunlight came into view, Orpheus glanced quickly over his shoulder—just to be sure.

Oh yes, it was Eurydice. Those eyes, that hair, that sweet mouth calling his name: "*Orpheus!*"

She sank down like a drowning swimmer: "Orpheus, why?" She fell back down and the darkness swallowed her up.

"Eurydice!"

But she was gone. Orpheus had lost his beloved a second time.

*

Orpheus was so broken-hearted that he could never again play cheerful music. When he touched his lyre, the notes sobbed out of it like tears.

"Play us something jolly, can't you?" demanded his audiences. But Orpheus played the only music he could. "Something jolly, we said!" And when he would not, they attacked him—and finally killed him.

His soul rushed out of his body, eager to reach the gloomy Underworld. "Let me go down to Eurydice!" he cried. "Surely I can, now that I'm dead?"

But the gods replied, "You shan't go down to the Underworld, Orpheus. Your music has given us such pleasure that your lyre shall be turned into stars and hung up in the night sky."

"But . . . " began Orpheus.

"And you shall live out eternity in that special place reserved for those loved by the gods. And Eurydice shall live there with you."

So the two spirits floated hand in hand to the Fields of Eternal Happiness, to sing and make music together for ever.

Atalanta's Race

On the island of Cyprus, in a lovely garden tended by Venus, the goddess of love, there grew an apple tree. It had yellow branches and yellow leaves, but its apples were glittering gold.

Now, in the days when that tree was in fruit, there lived a beautiful girl called Atalanta. Men had only to see her to fall in love with her, but she had sworn never to marry. The young men pestered her to change her mind and grew tiresome. So she declared, "I will only marry the man who can race against me and *win*. But anyone who tries—and fails—must agree to die."

Despite the risk, many young men wanted to race Atalanta to win her hand. But she could run like the wind. The runners tried and the runners died, because they came in second.

A young man named Hippomenes had heard of Atalanta's races. He thought any boy must be stupid to throw his life away on a silly dare. But when one day Atalanta streaked by him, brown and fast as a darting bird, he knew at once that he had to race for her.

When Atalanta saw Hippomenes, she did not want him to challenge her. He was too young and handsome to die. She half wanted him to win . . . but no! She had sworn never to marry.

A crowd gathered, impatient for another race, but Atalanta kept them waiting as she fretted about the result. And Hippomenes said his prayers.

"Oh, Venus!" prayed Hippomenes. "You plainly made me love this woman. So help me to win her!"

Venus heard him. She also thought Hippomenes too young and handsome to die. So she picked from the tree in her garden three golden apples and gave them to him. Now he was ready for the race.

*

"*Ready, steady, go!*" cried the starter.

Away went Hippomenes, as fast as he had ever run. Away went Atalanta, quick as a blink. She soon took the lead.

So Hippomenes threw one golden apple—beyond her, over her head. It caught the light. Atalanta ran to where it lay and picked it up. Hippomenes sped ahead.

But Atalanta caught him up again and passed him, hair blowing like a flag. He ran faster than any of the other suitors, but it was not fast enough.

So Hippomenes threw another of the apples. Again Atalanta stopped to pick it up and again Hippomenes took the lead. But Atalanta was so much faster that she could stop, admire, pick up the shiny apples and *still* catch him up again.

Hippomenes ran faster than any man has ever run, but it was not fast enough. So he threw the third apple. Would Atalanta be fooled by the trick a third time? She saw—she slowed down—she glanced at the two apples in her hands ... And she stopped for the third. The crowd cheered as Hippomenes dashed past her, lungs bursting, and threw himself over the winning line. He had won his bride!

And for a champion runner who has just lost a race for the first time Atalanta looked extremely happy.

The Wooden Horse

There was once a woman who hatched from an egg, like a bird. But she was more beautiful than any bird who ever flew. She was called Helen and there was not a prince, nor a duke, nor a king who did not want to win her. But she married old King Menelaus and lived in a palace on the shores of his kingdom.

If only that had put an end to the hopes of all the other princes, dukes and kings! Young, handsome Paris, Prince of Troy, found Helen too beautiful to forget, and wanted too much to have her for his own. So he stole Helen's love and ran away with her to Troy—the city called the City of Horses.

King Menelaus grieved—but his grief then turned to anger—and, calling together an army of fifty thousand men, he sailed for Troy to get back his wife. He took with him the greatest heroes of the world: Achilles the brave, Odysseus the cunning, and Ajax the proud. A thousand ships put ashore outside the tall white walls of Troy.

Helen looked out of her palace window and saw the fleet approaching. "What will happen now?" she wondered. "Who will win me? Which side do I *want* to win?"

For weeks, for months, for years the Greeks lay siege to the city. The great heroes of Troy fought in single combat with the great heroes of Greece, sword against sword, chariot against chariot. But it decided

nothing. After ten years, Achilles the brave was dead. Ajax the proud lay in a grave covered with flowers. And Paris too was dead and his lips too cold for kissing. So many good men had been killed. And those who had lived were sadder, wearier, older. Only Helen remained as lovely as ever—a precious prize locked inside Troy.

At last Odysseus the cunning spoke up. "I think I know how we can get inside the city of Troy." The Greeks listened eagerly.

"It'll never work!" said some.

"It's too dangerous!" said others.

But old King Menelaus nodded and said, "Do it, Odysseus."

For days the Trojans, inside their walls, could hear nothing but sawing and hammering.

Then one morning they looked over their high walls and saw . . . a horse. A huge wooden horse.

They also saw that the Greeks had packed up their tents, launched their ships and set sail. "They've gone! They've gone!" cheered the Trojans. "We've won the war! . . . But what's this they've left behind? A horse?" They crept outside to look.

"It's a tribute to Troy!" said some. "A tribute to the City of Horses!"

"It's a trick," said others.

One old man threw a spear at the wooden horse and it struck with a hollow thud. "Beware of Greeks even when they give you presents!" he warned.

But the people of Troy would not listen. "Don't be so dismal! The war's over! The Greeks have gone, haven't they?"

They began to celebrate, to drink wine and to dance. And they towed the huge wooden horse, on long ropes, in through the gates of Troy.

*

Meanwhile, inside the horse's hollow body, a dozen Greek soldiers crouched as still as stones. There was so little room in their hiding place that they were all pressed together, knee against knee, elbow against ear.

"Heave!" cried the Trojans, as they pulled the giant horse into the city square. The bumpy ride jogged and bruised the men hidden inside, but they held their breath and gripped their swords tight. One sneeze and they would be found out!

Helen looked out of her window and saw the horse, all decorated now with flowers and ribbons. She was a Greek and knew the ways of the Greeks and she thought to herself, "This is a trick." She turned away from the window, put a finger to her lips and sat quite still, waiting.

The happy Trojans danced all day round the long legs of the wooden horse. At last, weary with joy, they tottered home to sleep, and the city fell silent.

Then a secret door creaked open in the stomach of the horse. Down dropped a knotted rope. Down the rope climbed the dozen Greeks.

Meanwhile, the whole Greek fleet of ships sailed back to shore: they had only been hiding over the sea's horizon, waiting. As they pelted up the beach, they peered through the early morning darkness at the high, heavy city gates, anxious to see whether their plan had succeeded.

And there! The gates creaked open to let them in and the Greeks dashed through, swords at the ready. A war that had lasted ten years was over. They set light to Troy's tall buildings. They killed Troy's young men. Then they seized Helen and sailed away. By morning there was nothing but the sound of weeping within Troy's charred and crumbling walls.

And Helen lived once more in the palace of King Menelaus on the shores of his kingdom. If she had loved Paris once, she never said so, and never spoke his name, and she and Menelaus lived happily ever after.

Odysseus

The war was over at last. At last, after ten long years, the soldiers who had fought in it could sail home. Among them was Odysseus, King of Ithaca. He and his men rowed out to sea on their ship the *Odyssey*, leaving the battlefields far behind them.

There was little room aboard for food and water, but some huge jugs of wine stood in the prow, taken from the defeated enemy. Unfortunately, the first time they tasted it, the men fell asleep over their oars. "A bit too strong," decided Odysseus, watching them snore. Then a storm overtook them and blew them off course—to an island, who knows where?

Odysseus pointed up at a cliff. "I'm sure those caves up there are inhabited. Let's climb up and ask for directions and a bite to eat. Leave your swords here, and bring a jug of wine, to show we're friendly."

The first cave they came to was huge and smelled of cheese. But nobody was in. A fire burned in one corner. The soldiers sat down and waited. Soon there was a clatter of hoofs on the cliff path, as the island shepherd drove his flock home from the fields to the caves. And what sheep entered the cave! They were as big as cows, with fleeces like snowdrifts.

But the shepherd made his sheep look tiny. He was as big as the wooden horse of Troy, and his hair hung down like creepers. A single eye winked in the centre of his forehead. He rolled a massive boulder across the cave mouth, then turned and saw his visitors.

"Supper!" he roared, in delight. And picking up a man in each paw, he gobbled them down and spat out their belts and sandals.

"Sir! We came to you in peace! How dare you eat my men!" cried Odysseus, more angry than afraid.

"I'm Polyphemus the Cyclops," said the one-eyed giant. "I eat who I want. Who are you?"

"I am O . . . I am called No One—and I demand that you let us go! Why ever did I bring a present to a man like you?"

"Present? Where? Give it! I won't eat you if you give me a present!"

Odysseus pointed out the jug of wine.

Polyphemus chewed off the seal and gulped down the wine. He smacked his lips. "Good stuff, No One. Good stuff."

"So you'll roll back the boulder and let us go?"

"Oh, I wouldn't shay that," slurred the Cyclops, reeling about. "What I meant to shay wash, I won't eat you . . . till morning." And hooting with drunken laughter, he crashed down on his back, fast asleep.

Twelve men pushed against the boulder, but they could not roll it aside.

"We're finished, captain!" they cried.

But Odysseus was busy with the huge shepherd's crook—sharpening the end to a point with his knife. The work took all night.

Towards dawn, the sailors heated the point red-hot in the fire, lifted it to their shoulders ... and charged! They plunged the crook into the Cyclops' one horrible eye.

Polyphemus woke with a scream that brought his fellow giants running. "Polyphemus, what's wrong? Is there someone in there with you?"

"No One's in here with me!" groaned Polyphemus.

"Are you hurt, then?"

"No One has hurt me!" bellowed Polyphemus.

"Good, good," said the giants outside, and plodded back to their caves. "Perhaps he had a nightmare," they said.

Polyphemus groped about blindly. "Trickery won't save you, No One. You and your men shan't leave this cave alive!"

In the morning he rolled the boulder aside, so that his sheep could run out to the fields and feed. But he himself sat in the doorway, his hands spread to catch any Greek trying to escape.

Quickly, Odysseus told his men to cling on under the huge, woolly sheep, and although Polyphemus stroked each fleece as it came by him, he did not feel the man hanging on underneath.

So captain and crew escaped. But Odysseus called out as his ship sped past the cliff: "Know this, Polyphemus! It was I, the hero Odysseus, who blinded you! Remember the name!"

The Cyclops picked up boulders and hurled them down, hoping to sink the little boat. "Remember it? Know this, Odysseus! I am Polyphemus, son of Poseidon the sea god. And I call on my father to destroy you!"

Deep in the ocean, Poseidon heard his son's voice, and his angry storms drove the *Odyssey* even further off course—to a beautiful island carpeted with flowers.

A house stood at the top of the beach. The crew of the *Odyssey* ran up to it, and a woman welcomed them inside. But for some reason, Odysseus hung back. Only after the door was shut did he peep in at the window.

The woman brought each sailor bread, honey and wine. She carried a golden wand, and as she circled the table she rubbed it across their heads.

One by one, the men began to change. Their faces grew whiskery, their noses flat. They dropped the bowls, for their hands were changing into bony hoofs. One by one they rolled out of their chairs ... because pigs cannot easily sit up to table.

Pigs! Circe the enchantress had turned them into pigs! Now she drove them out of the back door and into her sties, where many other pigs squealed miserably.

Outside Odysseus searched among the flowers at his feet. He stooped down to pick one particular tiny white flower, put it into his mouth, then went boldly up to the house.

"Come in! So happy to see you!" Circe's voice was as sweet as her face. She brought Odysseus bread, honey and wine. He ate the bread and honey and drank the wine. Then Circe came and stood behind him and rapped him with her golden wand. "Now get to the sty with the rest of the pigs."

"Did you know," said Odysseus, calmly taking a tangle of petals out of his mouth, "that this flower is proof against magic potions?"

Circe struck him again. But she saw that her charms were powerless.

"Odysseus!" she said. (She knew his name: that startled him.) "A fortune-teller once foretold that I would be out-tricked by one Odysseus, King of Ithaca. You are my fate! I lay my magic and my heart at your feet."

"Just turn those pigs back into men," said Odysseus.

Circe ran and thrust her golden wand into each pig's pink ear, and in moments the yard was crowded with shivering men on hands and knees.

"Now will you love me?" Circe begged.

"My wife, Penelope, is waiting for me at home," said Odysseus. But for one whole year he stayed on Circe's island.

Then one day he went to Circe and said he must leave for home.

"It's such a dangerous voyage!" she sobbed. "You must pass the singing hideous sirens and then the whirlpool Charybdis . . . But if you must go, listen carefully and do exactly as I tell you."

Circe told Odysseus and his men to plug their ears with wax so as not to hear the song of the sirens. But Odysseus was curious to hear the famous singers. After setting sail, he told his men to rope him to the mast. And he did not plug his ears.

As the last knot of rope was tied, a sort of music came floating across the ocean.

"Circe lied. These sirens aren't hideous at all," thought Odysseus when an island came into view. "They're beautiful! Untie me, men, and let me swim over and speak to them!"

But his men could not hear him. The sirens' singing grew sweeter: its loveliness almost burst Odysseus' heart.

"Untie me!" he cried. "You go on, if you like, but I must stay. These ladies need me. Listen! They're calling me! Let me go!"

But his men could not hear him, and as the boat sailed away from the island, the singing grew softer.

"What did you see?" asked Odysseus.

"Vultures with women's heads, perched on a rock," said his friends. "And the bones of a thousand dead sailors."

Then Odysseus knew that Circe had not lied.

He also knew that a worse danger lay ahead: Charybdis.

Charybdis was more than a whirlpool. It was a great sucking mouth in the face of the ocean, in the shadow of a cliff. Twice a day it sucked in everything floating within seven miles of it. Twice a day it spewed out the wreckage. But thanks to Circe's advice, the men of Ithaca raced past Charybdis at the safest time of day and came to no harm at all.

But the sea god Poseidon's revenge was not over. His storm horses drove the *Odyssey* back, back, back, towards that terrible gaping mouth. The soldiers just had time to say goodbye to each other before their ship slipped over the glassy rim. For a moment it hung in mid-air. Odysseus leapt on to the stern, sprang upwards, and caught hold of a little bush growing on the cliff. Down fell his ship and men into the raging whirlpool beneath.

For four aching hours Odysseus clung to that bush, soaked with spray and deafened by roaring water. Then the tide filled Charybdis and stilled the whirling water. Broken pieces of his ship floated to the surface. Odysseus dropped down, clung to a plank of wood, and floated away across the sea.

For nine more years Odysseus had to travel the oceans from island to island, until at last he found help and friendship and a ship to carry him home to Ithaca.

*

Meanwhile Penelope waited patiently for her husband's return. Each day she watched at the window, but Odysseus did not come.

Others did. Idle, greedy young princes came calling on Penelope. "Odysseus must have drowned on his way home from the war," they said. "Marry one of us instead."

"I will wait a little longer," said Penelope politely.

But as the years passed, the visitors became less charming. "Choose, lady, or we will for you. Ithaca needs a king."

"Very well," said Penelope at last. "Let me weave a wedding veil. When it's finished, I will choose a new husband."

But although Penelope worked all day at her loom, the veil never seemed to be finished. Months passed and it had hardly grown at all. And why? Because every night, while her unwelcome suitors were snoring, Penelope crept out of bed and unpicked her needlework.

Then one night she was found out. One of the suitors found her at her loom, unpicking the threads by candlelight. "Enough!" he snarled. "Tomorrow you'll choose a husband, like it or not."

*

The ship bound for Ithaca with Odysseus aboard set sail while Poseidon was dozing. Imagine the sea god's fury when he woke and saw Odysseus, his hated enemy, sleeping safe and sound on an Ithacan beach.

Poseidon punished the ship that had helped Odysseus reach home—seized it and cursed it into stone. There it stands, to this day, a narrow ship of rock with stone rowers bending over stony oars. The seagulls perch on it and shriek.

The day came when Penelope must choose a new husband from among the greedy princes. A great feast was arranged. But the unhappy queen ate none of the food laid in front of her. "If only he had come," she thought.

The suitors crammed their mouths and drank themselves drunk.

Outside in the yard lay an old dog—Odysseus' old hunting dog. He got nothing but kicks and cuffs from the princes. His bones showed through his dull coat, and his eyes were blind. Just then, a ragged old beggar shuffled into the yard and sat down. The dog raised his head and sniffed—and got up and tottered towards the sound of a familiar voice.

"Hello, old friend. You remember me, don't you?" The dog laid his head in the beggar's lap and, content at last, died with his head between loving hands.

The beggar shuffled into the hall where the feast was in progress. At one chair after another he begged a bite of food, a sup of wine. "I'm a poor unfortunate sailor, shipwrecked on these shores. Spare me a little something."

But the suitors drove him away with slaps and kicks. Only Queen Penelope asked him to eat the food set in her place. "Somewhere on his journeys my husband, Odysseus, may have asked for help from strangers. I hope he found at least one heart to pity him."

"Odysseus?" jeered the suitors. "He's dead and gone! Choose! It's time for you to choose one of us!" And they thumped the table. "Choose! Choose! Choose!"

"Very well." Penelope spoke with quiet dignity. "You shall compete for my hand. And this is the task I set. Put your axes on the table, head down. See how each one has a thong on its handle? Well, I shall marry the first man who can fire an arrow directly through all those thongs . . . using the dead king's own bow."

The suitors swept the food off the table. They snatched Odysseus' hunting bow off the wall and struggled to string it. But though they grunted and strained, they could not bend the bow.

"Allow me," said the beggar, and bent it as though it were willow, and strung it. The suitors kicked him into a corner.

Then each tried to fire an arrow through the thongs of the axes. They all failed and cursed and argued. The axes tumbled a hundred times.

Penelope got up to leave the hall.

"May I try?" asked the beggar.

"Get away, you filthy creature," said a prince. "This contest is for the hand of a queen!"

"Let him try," said Penelope. "I'd as soon marry a penniless beggar as any one of you." And she closed the door behind her.

But once the beggar had the bow in his hands, he did not take aim on the axes. He leapt on to the table and fired one arrow after another—into the hearts of the suitors.

"Hear this and die!" he shouted. "Odysseus has returned to rid his palace of rats and toads!"

Penelope heard the fighting and thought the suitors must be quarrelling again. At last, silence. Her son came running to find her. "He's outside! He's killed them all, Mother! He's home! After all these years, Father has come home!"

Penelope went down to the hall. There stood Odysseus, his disguise thrown off and his face washed. "Welcome, sir," she said rather coldly. "You must be weary. I'll have a bed made up for you."

Odysseus' heart sank. Had Penelope's love died during the twenty years he had been away? "I'd rather sleep in my own bed, lady," he said timidly.

"Very well. I shall have it carried to the east chamber."

A spark twinkled in Odysseus' eye. "How could you move our bed when it's carved out of the very tree which holds up the room of this palace?"

When Penelope heard his words, she fell into Odysseus' arms and kissed him. "I had to be sure it was you. And only you could know about our bed!" she said. "Welcome home, Odysseus!"

Freedom for Prometheus

Even the gods grow wiser as they grow older. Almighty Zeus, king of the gods, looked down one day from Mount Olympus and saw Prometheus still chained to his rock, condemned for ever to be tortured by eagles. Zeus felt a kind of shame, because it is shameful for the strong to bully the weak.

And he felt a kind of pity, because it is sad to see a father kept from his children, an artist kept from his handiwork.

And he felt a kind of admiration: not just for Prometheus for enduring his pain, but for the little men and women Prometheus had made out of water and mud. If he had not given them the gift of fire, how could there be fires burning now on a thousand altars throughout the world, raising up holy, sweet-scented smoke to heaven?

For all they were cheeky and ugly and caught cold and grew old and stole and quarrelled and made mistakes and died, there were heroes and heroines among those men and women.

So Zeus broke Prometheus' chains with pliers of lightning, and wrapped the eagles in whirlwinds and spun them away to the four corners of the world. And Prometheus was free once more to champion the little people of the world, whom he had made out of water and mud.